published 2021

Northern Undercurrents

ISBN 978-0-9958247-9-9

cover artwork by Lea-Ann Dorval

Dedicated to the fierce,
loving adventure that is
Joanna Macy

and to all my courageous
loved ones.

Peaceweaver,
may I hold my threads of fear
in gentle hands,

caress with breath
these pains

and bring them into day
where others may see.

My base desires
- so beautiful –
for air and water,
kindness and food,
winkings of joy and belonging,
safety to rest on the ground

are deeply shared
underneath our forgetting

these strands of gratitude
in our hands,
tapestries of choices.

Birthpangs of sorrow,
this flow of tears
clenching my days
with quiet moans of awareness

deep sighs of ungood

regret and dis-ease
snowballing
where I used to breathe free.

Contractions
of a heart that knows joy,
of eyes that were clear
and now cloudy

a womb no longer fertile
like it was,

the rip and tear
of private skin
stretching and too stretched,
labia of lifetimes

opening in surrender,
learning to bear down
in gaia time.

Veils,
or wet onion skins,
these thin unfurlings

membranes of water and air
denoting separations

porous beings all

these delicate delineations
have no meaning

our pulsings
entwined with gravity and moon,
intestinal biospheres,
awareness crossing bodies and time.

I held out hope
for healthy boundaries

never imagining
this fragile shimmer.

A hesitance of now,
dipping my toe
in the moment

like standing
in a hurricane
winds spinning

with one foot reaching
to the quiet centre

the rest of me
accustomed
to storm.

May I let myself
fall forward,
collapse out of norm

pause
in a heap

a tranquil mess
receiving grace

knowing the winds still howl,

lengthening
a dignified spine.

She asked me
"are you done?"

and baby, I'm just getting started

this rant
an invitation

to dance while our house is burning,
to haul water
and save what we can

not pretending we will work
without grime on our faces
or desperate thirst

but stomping our feet
in shared rhythms,
turning our anger to power

wild ululations
saving our home.

Kinnikinick undervalued,
underfoot,
unseen in plain view everywhere

how I have disdained
to notice
your sturdy leaves
ready to soften my fall,
a cushioning of earth.

How I turned my nose
from the powdery flesh of your berries,
preferring the juicy red of your cousin,
ignoring your sweet flowering each spring.

I didn't see
your spread and reach,
uplifted leaves stretching towards sun,
crawling outwards in widening circles.
I didn't see your inherent resolve,
weathering each winter, a hidden green.

Now, in the belly-pain of days,
when my only courage
is to lie facedown in your embrace,
I thank you
for this proximity.

The sand moves under my left foot, sinking a little as I bend to pick up sticks. I've been clearing brush, a little each day, watching the changes on the path of sand between the new well and the cabins. Boreal forest scraped away by machines so we could trench in the water lines. Pine branches with prickly bark, some needles still green, others dark rust. Poplar branches, leaves curled paper in the sun. My foot, sinking slightly where the residue of change is still unsettled. Dry seeds of grasses I scattered a month ago, still on the surface of the sand except closer to the cabins where I watered. The way natural poplar shoots, these miniature trees, have started filling in the sandy swath, also vetch and crocus and kinnikinnick stretching outwards. I helped a little, a basin of pansies bright orange and purple where the driveway used to be, a small barricade of stones protecting the green shoots where the hose could reach.

Too much change for me to water well, too little rain. And yet still the growing is happening, resilience in action despite my plans, diverse little plants and lichens I don't have names for, white-green curlicues of barely visible arms stretching for sun, drinking whatever random droplet of water happens to fall. How the ground is alive, how wildly obvious the diversity of lifeforms in what looks like a patch of sand with flecks of green, how a month seems long and dry and at the end of it there is so much to show for it even with no effort, this wonder my only gift to give, this lush desert impossibly dry and wet at the same time. Fireweed, magenta spears emerging from disturbed ground.

Pace of a leaf
unfurling

not time-lapse dance

but real time;

may I slow,

feel organic day,

hear rain drip off the eave.

And all the while

a leaf

receiving, grows

no effort

just a widening spread

shaped by light and wet

happening,

pace of a leaf.

Love letters,
how we curve the alphabet

or nowadays tap

shaping words
an art form
of the everyday

expressing
all this need
and the kindness that is truth

synergy
fundamental to language

an evolution
reminding us of whale song

of all that we've forgotten

remembered.

Befriending time,

a quest, adventure

in my battling,

rising and falling

in the flood of it.

Trying too hard,

cramming a day,

eye on the horizon

of this finitude,

these numbered breaths;

befriending

the welcome of this one,

expanding lung

to hug my heart.

Sun warming my skin,
this fresh breeze
percussioned by poplar
like a brush
sliding on a drum

birdsong and joy
melodic on my ease

with a bellyful
of cloud, dark shame
rising

the taste of it bitter.

O wind, and nurturing sun
that cares at precise distance

may I open my jaw
for warming,
let the breath of the world
stroke away this ancient miasma

old stories lifted
freed by daylight,
exposed as empty air,
received by swaying trees.

The apartment is alive with a menagerie of sounds. The tap drips into the kitchen sink like a long leggy stork, stomping. Tin on the outside walls creaks like an old tree limb, the rustlings of wind as birds' wings in constant motion, a faint reminder of how nests are protection, the gift of being inside.

Radiator heat pulses through the edge of the floor, a snake pushing, causing the earth to crack, shift, change in response to its flow.

Perched at the top of the stairs like a noisy cage, this place I've come for refuge reminds me that real oases are like this, cacophonies of creatures slurping at life.

Soup to nuts
the whole meal

specific cans,
a label large
on the gallery wall

resonance
in the mundane.

Dust on a bedside lamp,
two small oranges huddled
after travelling the ocean
to be consumed

unread books
pulling like magnets,
portals to new vistas

obsolete detritus
to the uninitiated

may I unclutter my eyes.

To notice
gently
the gap

- breath enters flute,
moving in silence

before emergent sound.

I did the best I could
and yes
that won't be enough
to protect me from shame

it still found me
in the flesh

all the wobbly bits
untended

the times I recoiled
from life,

all the wishing.

And here I slither,
part reptile

like all of us,

wearing a skin too small,

feeling the flex of underneath new,

same rock sometimes warmed by sun.

Did the river
change direction

have I been lying
on the bank

facing the wrong way

or staggering wet
upstream

trying to find my feet
?

Is it me
who shifted

to be carried downstream,
my force a rudder
instead of a pole

or did some wild geology
find expression in time,
altering the current
?

The foamie in the back of the minivan didn't quite mask the bumps on the floor where the seats had been removed. Early August, the sky was still light near midnight, making it harder to sleep. But mostly it was the stimulation of being with women around the campfire, adrenalin still in her veins, stories replaying. A mug of wine, a gathering of grey hair. Adventures retold, the women who'd been river guides, the one who was embarrassed to have put an axe through her foot. Stories of bears. Stories of the front line when the cops refused to put themselves at risk and women stepped in. Stories of women who left husbands, whose husbands left them. Of shedding children as they aged. Of packing up and moving north and starting over. Foraging spruce tips and pickling them to share. Art shows held in foreign countries years ago, and art shows last week for the very first time. Women from rural Yukon who knew Whitehorse as the big city. Women from Toronto who knew Whitehorse as a remote village. Favourite sweaters decades old. An old camper bus newly acquired. The howling of dog teams. More than a millennium of experience around one campfire, accompanied by aspen waves. No wonder she couldn't sleep.

Dark pelt
this night

soft silence no moon
pinpricks of old passages,
travelled through billions of years,
tiny silver blessings
dotting the sky.

A light-year,
and millions of them,
stretching like wingtips
caressing our earth,
a dance of spectrum and time,
eyesight
and other perceiving.

No story required,
the uncertain dark
wraps the need to walk,
slows stumbling

these starlights
ineffable.

Waifs and adolescents

clamouring

my nighttime cacophony,

untended me

competing for attention,

body rigid

with all the vibrations.

May I stretch

to soften,

release all hope

in exchange for kindness,

honour the mess.

Sweat and freeze,
drip and shiver,
I stumble gracefully,
stride with uncertainty.

Creative bodies
wiser than mine
send shafts of light
to pierce my fog

and I with reverence
bow
to what they're learning

my wonder
a gift
to their beauty,
a breath
under their wings,
a moment to life mine.

Almond of my heart,
the press of days
squeezes slowly

and yes this is a death
to form and familiar,

a terror of love
transforming.

Sages point to this pain
with gnarled fingers

and all my hoping
for another route
has withered

reluctance melting into welcome

grinding weight compressing who I was

a forced breathing,
unbearable pressure

a whiff of sweet oil.

Violet

violin

violent

violation…

may I open this body

and this pierced heart

to the pain of all women,

the soft acknowledgment

of shared shame,

the bonds of fear

surrendered

to chains of fierce joy,

these golden links of love.

I feel uncomfortable
every single day

not just once
but often

and will feel discomfort
as long as I breathe
on this good earth.

Cold and wet
will find me

and heat and sweat

with shame
and hours of resentment

with sweet hungry longings
and flashes of bright

soft enfoldings of cloud

avalanches of pain

nectars of joy

beautifully raw.

Pruning,

I act

to protect my house,

cut what abrades

so it falls to ground,

trimming wild growth

to stop the knocking,

removing excess

to sustain what is here.

There's another kind of joy

after falling to ground,

relief in every pore

as tears soak earth

and she embraces

with gravity,

magnetism holding us close.

These places

where we fall no farther

even as we spin in space,

expansive grief broken open

to new gladness,

nose in soil.

When my cramped heart
says no

may I place it gently
in the heart of the world

bathing my fears

trusting a larger love
evolving us all.

My petty crises melt,
my anxious love that poisons a day
dissolves

in the generous laugh,
the heart of the world

more varied and precise
than this little mind,

impossible joy
flowing anyway.

Once there was a woman who found a vivid patch of magenta roses growing in a little clearing. It was a place in the woods that had just enough sun and rain to nurture some seeds that a bird dropped decades ago.

She looked at this abundance of roses, glowing their natural range of pinks in this unexpected place in the forest. She considered whether she could take one and decided to try. She had no knife but went to the stems carefully, selecting a flower with sharp thorns. The stem had a smooth patch near its roots, unprotected, vulnerable, that made it available to her. She bent the stalk, folding and twisting it until it broke free. She got poked in the process, but the flower's petals stayed bright and beautiful, and the scent filled her body with pleasure.

She was careful in how she handled it, carrying it home with reverence and joy.

As she approached, she could see her beloved on the deck, smoking. She called out: "Is this a good time to show you something beautiful?"

"Sure, I'd love to see it."

As she drew closer, he panicked. "Thorns!" he yelled. He raced to her and grabbed the flower, stabbing himself in the hand.

"You're trying to hurt me!" he wailed, stomping on the threat, wounding his bare feet. Blood trickled from his palms as he raised them to her, backing away.

"I can't believe you brought me thorns," he snarled. "Can't you see I've had a bad day?"

Two small flowers
growing like weeds

prolific and messy

adorning a resonant bowl,

a handcrafted conduit of love
made with deep care
that travelled north
to sing
when touched by practiced hands.

Two separate flowers
moved by the pulse of a room
and ground underneath it,
vibrations of harmony
and discord
shaking them free
of barriers

nestling together
in a world gone mad,
in a world suffused with tenderness

joined in new strength,
receiving alignment;
attunement of tones
nurturing.

Verdant,
there is snow
and time until planting

but my blood
feels rich today

flow and possibility
swelling my thin skin

flushing dry lands
where I've lingered

and though there is no green
in these white vistas

I can hear the sound of lush.

A quickening,
may I rest
just enough
to catch my breath

to let it fly
with all that needs release

to welcome it back home.

May I rest
just enough
for a twinkle in my eye
to dance
across these wrinkled lines

not looking
for plump beauty,
the energy of youth

but just enough
to fuel my laughing mouth,
shake off cobwebs,
spin new silk.

All living
is perception

I like this word
as a bell

sounding my reminder

I am a filter
receiving

my shaped and shifting views,
clogged and cleaned

a bio-receptor
created to notice

all that is

an energy stream of realness
made illusory
through my filtering

necessary, inevitable
limitations

and permeable,

beloved adventure
in the never-sure.

Today's anger is about inaction, rage at myself for being in this mess, for letting myself be a target of blame, for the ways I can't control the decisions of others and struggle to enact my own choices. And there's an urge to act in some big way, make some choice that will put my world to rights, put me back on course. But as I imagine my choices – moving out, shutting the farm, getting a new job, travelling to water, escaping with a friend – they get more diaphanous, luminescent, shimmering like the fantasies produced by dehydration in a desert. And the water of realness comes back to quench my thirst, the gratitude for what is actually here, the way that everything happening today is enough, that the panic and urgency are the delusions.

I will act. I will continue to choose dignity and respect, even when there are threats. I will continue to soften my drama, drink tea, bring my attention to what is here, my feet on this mottled carpet, the sounds of young men hauling brush with the ATV trailer. My most significant act these days is a full exhale. And noticing how leaves move with no volition of their own.

Daughter of Sue and Ross,
granddaughter to Grant, Nicol, Margaret
and Inez,
wife to Andrew
mother of Jacob and Sam

I honour
the inukshuks of my way

names that place me.

And o my loved friends and neighbours,

kind faces of my kin

marking my territory,

enclosure

a word I used to chafe against;

now tenderness enfolds

the realness

of my place in time.

The same day the rainbow
lay flat against mountain,
lounging on top of the greenhouse

I saw the eagle
huge

swirling its prophecy
in large circles of care

greetings from beloveds
it knows by name

even though the names are shed.

It flew high
over the place I call home,
a confident majesty of space
in the spirals
traced by its torso
fueling wings
using precision to rest in air
and keep moving.

May I learn from this grace
how to rest wisely in currents,
precise in my choices
so I can ride
what carries me.

Embrace of tomorrow,
we all imagine
there will be one

rationing love
as if it needs to last

honey in a closet

a saved grace
like an RSP

illusory protection.

Today
may I love naked,

offer sweetness even to me,

especially to all
when I urge to avert my gaze

cellulite and scars,
real acne

the balm of love
healing this last day.

A pink blessing
tinged with purple

light filtered
through sacred feminine

a convent
repurposed

arms of women
holding in circle

my mentor
blessing my forearm
with her grip

the music
of a loved traveller
bathing us all

wounded bodies
and so much strength

light
embodied

pink suffusing
love

imbuing
a natural authority
to act.

There's a cardboard box on the floor; it's filled with items she's loaned me. An ironed tablecloth is folded on top of the pile, white and pale blue. I can see the edge of a Ziploc bag that holds essential oils for her diffuser. She knows how to make the cabins look and smell lovely. She loves to help in practical ways; covid shutdown made it hard for her to engage with others, bring them baking or handmade gifts.

There's a remnant of tape on the edge of the box. When I turn my head just a little, the light shines on this fragment and it sparkles, like a flash on a lake. This particular tilt of this head at this moment, the convergence of my height and my slouch and the dim overhead light and a random old piece of tape. No one else could see it, nor can I when I shift my posture. How many miniature miracles we forget to notice. How we can't create them, just pay attention to the happening. A flash of light where one is unexpected.

If onlys
matted
like long hair ignored

too long free from care
tangled without intention

dread-locked
past time to disentangle

may shears
be wielded gently

releasing new health,
unfurling
a shortened span.

Sorrow
like a septic field
buried

the whiff of it
signalling need

deep ferment

a liquid inaccessible
without help

underground rising
transforming decadent shit.

I can't feel
the upwelling

but know it's there;

may it leach and filter
in good time.

Kickboxer

He mutters down the street,
propelled by rage

kicking out his foot
90 degrees

the lift of intensity,
jabbing his unseen attacker

so much fierce power.

And yes, we try to ignore
and stare
to mark our differences

use pity as distorted thanks
for our safer path,

no repetitive fury
fuming all day,
not wounded with such rupture.

Instead let me feel
the honour,
his liberation
from pretense,
wounds and valour on display

let me vibrate
with my own urges
to kick at what hurts,
to yell at my past
as if it could hear

ignoring what others
might not see

turning my rage
into strength,
a practicing

bowing to my teacher
in every thing.

It's the small things
that undo me

not large aches
and sacred disclosures,
doom or pestilence,
painful abuse

the friends who want to die
in the pain of it

by some large grace,
I find the scent of love

but oh,
this petty belly
stumbles

pinpricked by a lost key,
stabbed by a frozen ignition,
boiled-over soup,
missing file,
inflamed by injustice at customer service;

may I pause
in this angry field,
sniff the air.

Turn my sorrow
into soup

let me add to the pot
freely

all these vegetables
wrinkled in the fridge

cold and losing life;

may I slice cleanly,
discard what is mouldy
and past its best,

cry with the sting of onions,
cry with the shame
of all my yesterdays,
drip salt
like a resource

a flavouring,

my sorrow nourishing,

this stirring heat
transforming,

a savoury yum.

Not pearls
with their precious sameness

more like rainbows,
iridescent baubles
of soap

round colours of completeness
expanding with care,

with slow attention

to each day's

glistening.

We're lying on white sheets, white satin stripes on the duvet. Motel room queen bed, MacBook resting on my right knee and his left. My son. We're watching Murdoch Mysteries, a break from his other series, a retreat into the 1900s, imaginary softness of an earlier time.

Our motel room rendezvous feels illicit in this era of lockdown. I've boldly marched through 2 airports, rented a car, masked and sanitized my way to this reunion. His hair, the burnt copper of an old pan, a tarnished penny, how it hangs close to his ear when he takes off the baseball cap. How I reach out my hand during the episode, barely touch the auburn strand, how he catches my eye because he knows this is why I am here. No words. My right forefinger on his hair, two seconds. A pandemic of tender unspoken distance finding a hopeless ease. That copper colour.

Launched

as if I had anything to do with it

the way life stretches

these filaments of light
brighter and more distant.

He once lived tucked
beneath my heart

now his own galaxy orbits

a sunlight
that warms me.

A sandal track
in desert

Salopek following,

and me in snow

tracing my path,

bootprints

bare feet

trudging and dancing,

millennia and millions

tickling the planet,

may we walk gently.

Ferocity of care,
may this anger
like an oil slick
blocking sweet water

burn as fuel

contained by some new mushroom
ancient
a mycelial net
feeding on this dreck

flames vivid
in this black night

warning and beacon.

Those leaves,
all that fluttering
looking like activity

all those whirling parts

as if a tree
coordinates all that movement,
all day long

how silly
misunderstanding

leaves at rest
even as they spin

surrendered to breeze.

O yes
my greed

wanting rivers of justice

and dancings of people
in forests
and streets

swords to plows
and closing the factories of death

gently and firmly
intervening

these suicides of profit
redeemed,
coaxed off the ledge

our radioactive addictions,
oil and gas,
plastic ease,
sugar and palm,
caged cruelties of all kinds

brought into day
without blame,

just a wise tracing of pain,
tears melting our terror,
releasing our shared resolve.

Freud had it wrong,
I do not envy
an appendage

but rather the deep growls,
guttural violent sounds
that vibrate in other lives

scary fearful low notes,
lacerated power
unleashed in sound

the roaring of rage.

My own anger shrill
in my ears, bitter in my belly,
frustrated in salty tears
often with no noise
or none heard

may I growl like mama grizzly,
mother ocean's storm,
the cracking open of mountains,
boulders crashing down.

This deep love,
thwarted too long,
she rises fierce
from her hot core,
she rumbles her way
through the night,
calling her daughters
to lead their children,
sons and women
waking

howling their love
more deeply
than ever before.

Black moth
large inside belly
flapping soft wings of dark
terror
beating in my chest
much faster than my heart,
wingspan too broad
to escape through my throat.

This trapped creature
yearns to fly,
panic bruising its wings,

delicate strength
surging
in a hopeless space

confined
by walls it depends on

flapping a nauseous storm,
hurricanes of dread.

And so each breath,
a wider moan of mouth
gasping

a torrent of tears

cracking open a cavern

simple agony of birth.

"Have some fun," she said. And my mind started scrambling for a moment of fun, a recent laugh, a recent nourishing. All of it gallows humour, the smile of irony, shared understanding it could always be worse.

Rain on the tin roof, watering. How we need it, cold and wet, the flow of deep delayal of gratification. Leaves will come as the result of this rain. It doesn't feel fun. And there's a humour buried in this human reaction, the funny bone of our dissatisfaction, wanting some other reality that the one that can nourish us right now.

So much of my life is breaking apart, falling into decay, and I'd love to skip this painful season, to release this dark moth flying in my belly and chest.

Dukka

Title word pushes to brain

ignores the sacred pain
of intimacy,
the way my discontent
has resided so long
in fibres of my flesh

nerve endings fraught
with lack

decades of unloved moments
flooding these eyes
to trickle down wrinkled cheeks

fists raised against deep kinship

growls of inadequacy

turned heads, departures, doors closed.

Sneers of a lifetime,
wearing scars that become numb,

unresponsive to birdsong,
ears closed to joy.

Deep roots
in winter
warmer
for their depth

the buried earth
retaining heat

protecting the unseen.

So too
when we extend
our downwards reach,
relaxing fearful feet
to earth's embrace

stretching into dark

eyeless in the soil of days,

bitter wind
and tendrils held below,

a hug
of planet-time

a pause
as the axis keeps dipping to spring.

For so long
this collecting

pearls and fragrant blooms

textures and flavours

and wanting to share,

offering tastes of beauty
astringent and sweet

like an alms bowl filled

and how this too is lack,
a way of begging in the world.

Instead

like a basket of warm cookies

may I carry the pleasure of these crumbs,
savour their scents
and the ways I am fed,

open basket on offer,
pores alight in the walking.

The backhoe
scraped what was there
intact

now space for a home
that has sheltered us well

while earth,
left mostly untouched
after abrasion

took time to heal,

a cycling of snow and sun
through decades

raw sand
collecting seeds,
accumulating leaves each fall

and spring
shucks her wet skirt,
reveals her bloomers.

Heather's Wish List

is not a list
or wishes

because those she can do,
can bring forth,
catch like a midwife.

Her deepest glimmers
are flashes of dream

a dozen people
children and old
in white on the lawn,
moving chi

a circle of tears,
heartbreak and rage,
room for the pain
of being human

a blossoming of grandkids,
sons joyful

a land released into nurturing,
leaves reaching to sky
nourishing our soles and bellies and souls

a circle of minds
in service to heart,
plodding together
new paths,
our maps
the film of retrospect
for others to absorb

no maps forward.

The sky outside the window is blue with white clouds. Half an hour ago it was dark grey and dripping. I can't ask the weather to slow down, to let me relax into something more steady. The planet spins without my opinion or plea. My vertigo is from trying to slow down the change that is constant. Relaxing, I can feel myself a dry leaf on water, bumping into what is here, moving with the current. Many hard knocks, no problem.

This morning before the rain, I walked with the dog. Dark clouds, green pine needles and undergrowth but what kept drawing my eye were grey sticks on the ground, grey branches dead on living trees, grey stumps sculptured in repose.

A death walk but my heart was light, noticing the grey against the green, noticing the living trees with dead red needles among their green ones. Laughing at death not because we vanquish it, but because it is everywhere, accompanying. We need dead cells so we can grow new ones, slough ourselves off.

There was a grey sky mirroring the dead branches. And now that same sky is blue and white, sun warming the green.

These hearts
unwrapped,
a journey of right here,
a quest of breaths

each delicious
with its flavour

no big ideas,

very big sky.

Noah building an ark
while neighbours gawked

or Rumi
drunk with life,
staggering the dusty road

or even me
with this stunned look
and bedhead

while the planet
– her majesty –
dips her toe
to ripple my room.

Handcream
the smell of oranges
rubbed on my skin

rain outside reminding
of rise and fall

the upward flow unseen
and essential.

How the soft scent
from the pretty jar
was gifted

the woman mothering
a daughter

who is friend to the daughter
of my teacher faraway

how the girls
will turn my teacher's home
into a summer of laughter

and my teacher
will be free to roam

each object in my home
these filaments,
mycelium.

Sinews of sorrow
like a violin strung in fear,
taut wires
emanating screech

the bow of my heart
drawn unwieldy
on this body,

five decades of clenching
unintended

a lifetime of practice avoided.

Horror of waste,
a sad cacophony
of what never was,

may I walk this desolate plateau
void of arpeggio,

willing to soften
my shame,

learn a simple scale.

It's 1:48 am, the bedside lamp reveals. She sighs forcefully, not loud enough to wake anyone down the hall, throwing back the covers and swinging her feet to the floor. Her stomach clenches even further. The sigh released air she can't quite get back, some inexplicable math of depletion. The numbers on the clock keep moving. And everything inside her feels stuck and soiled, a sorrowing of tissue and bone. She feels her hips and knees rising, watches herself move to the door handle, the corridor, the kitchen sink. Pale dusk in the middle of this northern night. Her hand knocks the faucet on, fills the cup, turns off the flow. It rises to her lips and forces her to sip.

"Is this surrender?" she wonders. The deference of her will to her body, letting it lead while she admits her helplessness, haplessness, lack of volition. Feet on the floor, breathing. She feels the turbulent lifestream of facts, the choice to close her business, the dark raven of debt, the mental earthquakes that are causing him to cry whenever they try to talk about what's happening. How he literally cannot hear her through his tears, how hers keep freezing to keep something solid for this flow of events.

My worst nightmare
feels lodged in my belly

making it hard
to breathe in this day

an inhale blocked

by my powerless rage
lidded
because it is ridiculous

a dissonant boiling.

If a straw
did break a camel

then I understand
a lightweight email
crushing my bones

the dust of my resentments
sparked to fire

may even a faulty breath
cool this heat.

A decadence of lawn
gambolling
through busy summers,
boys on their backs
absorbing sky

soccer after supper

a humming of insects rising.

This year,
the hard winter
left patches of death

and voles trailed their hunger
to eat what was lush

and me on my knees with a knife
to root out dandelions,
pull fireweed

both of these flowers essential
past my boundary of green.

Love in this tending,
even though it is unnatural,
the real world growing more robust
past the edge of manicured sod,
flowers of wildness and diversity.

Near the river,
not just its width
but also how its depth
rolls my way

a fluid mountain

oft-forgotten power
beneath what we see.

My heart
robust and wide
opens to flows
of people and pain,
of meteors
flashing in descent
and travelling unseen in vacuum,

of plastic
in my garbage,

tenderness of photos,

a tumbling of boys.

Oracular,
a feminine flood
pervades,
exhorts a surrender
to fierce joy,
wild swirling.

Particulate,
these flashes of dust,
dirt and DNA discarded
on the floor,

a drudgery of tasks,
a constant incoherence
searching for resonant sound.

The blue scarf hangs in my room. It's cotton and rayon, silky, a deep blue like a child's crayon making a bright ocean. I can't remember where I bought it, but I do know I bought it for myself. One of the few items in my room that wasn't a gift.

I bought it to wear as a shawl, travelling somewhere with bare arms, and it was perfect. Casual, a little bit warm, knotted tassels making a fringe at each end. Pretty. Wrapping myself in a colour I love.

When Eleanor was in the nursing home, she was often chilly. The heating system blew cool air at her desk, and she asked if I could bring her a shawl. Of course I brought an armload, including the blue one. Anything she wanted, her light in my life like a nectar I drank whenever I could.

When she was planning her death, she asked if she could keep my shawl close. So many people loved her, my shawl was a proxy for me, as I couldn't be in her small circle at the end.

The beauty of assisted dying meant I could prepare. I sat in meditation with Andrew, wearing her red scarf, the one with all the little beads on the fringe. When she died, I felt her presence soar over my place, back to her home next door before moving on. The red beads broke and rattled on the floor.

Now the blue scarf is in my room. It was Sam's room before, and the scarf hangs over the cupboard where his camera gear still resides, his high school memorabilia. The hidden back of the scarf has her name in one corner, an institutional laundry tag that keeps things sorted for residents. My eyes drink the blue softness every day.

A neighbour
gone nuts
honestly

with sobs
and calls for help,
courage to fall on the floor

a businesswoman
with gracious tears of trauma
in the boardroom,
my own dripping

a friend
on the phone
who can't breathe
past the fear
squeezing her lungs

each of these steady
for so long

me in my leaky boat
I've cut holes in

may there be some reason
we drown.

This lazy me
stewing
in her ivory tower
that isn't

in her solitude
surrounded
by people to smile at

wasting
the gift of trees
pressed into paper

and whatever toxic gunk
they make ink of

… this mess
of ingested sugar
and microplastics
labelled "me"

as if there is any separation

this fury
with nowhere to go

and sorrow
a tsunami behind it

salty ferocious love.

The sky, deep rose and orange
petals of dawn
a laughing gardener
spilling her basket
across all the mountains,
petals of light on dark clouds
lit and shifting

and now she soars
beyond the clouds,
dark blanket of rain
washing early day

and though I am pierced
by the passing,
jubilation gone

I don't have to be.

When I sit here in bed,
propped up with pillows
against the wall,
coffee sustaining
this dread,
these liquid drops
sliding off my chin,
cramped belly
judging…
not even the dread
of porpoises dying
and how we breathe plastic,
but these petty vivisections
slicing my guts,
whether I can pay a bill,
or get through a day
without a fight,
or breathe five times
without pain
in this soft bed
where nothing is wrong.

There are ways I can fall
without refuge,
no safe landing,
no ground;
a trap door
in my belly
and they forgot
to tie the noose
and so the falling
feels endless,
empty lava tube
off-centre,
not through to someplace warm.

Despite terror, I breathe,
reminding me of otherness,
how air is reciprocal,
atmosphere requiring more than one,
so this black hole
is a lie, shared
by millions like me,
and trees.

The breathing YaxKasei

To watch you stand
at your own height,
solid feet on ground,
your young son's arm
around your shoulders

or dance for your cousin
as yourself,
love in every move

and hear you speak
of family adzed
into new beauty,
a towering alignment
as gift to all of us

makes tears of joy
slide on my skin,
celebrating your freedom
to wear your own name.

Bright flashes on water,
so too these bones
condensed
a form of light
like all solids
including the shape of me.

Vast distance
between cells
and supernovae
even farther

no air there for waves of sound
enforces silence

yet here
our sloshy breathing
with trees

creates a riotous band,
tapping ears.

Perhaps the scent of peppermint,
or skin on a dry morning
akin to lizards

or peeling one segment of orange
so soft ridges can rest
on your lumpy tongue

reminds you of this
light density.

www.ingramcontent.com/pod-product-compliance
Lightning Source LLC
Chambersburg PA
CBHW071928020426
42331CB00010B/2765